WRITTEN ON WATER

WRITTEN ON WATER

Michel Marc Bouchard

Translated by

Linda Gaboriau

TALONBOOKS
2004

Talonbooks
P.O. Box 2076, Vancouver, British Columbia, Canada V6B 3S3
www.talonbooks.com

Typeset in New Baskerville and printed and bound in Canada.

First Printing: January 2004

Les Manuscrits du déluge was published in the original French by Leméac Éditeur in 2003.

National Library of Canada Cataloguing in Publication Data
Bouchard, Michel Marc, 1958–
[Manuscrits du déluge. English]
   Written on water / Michel Marc Bouchard ; translated by Linda Gaboriau.
   A play.
   Traduction de: Les manuscrits du déluge.
   ISBN 0-88922-492-7
   I. Gaboriau, Linda II. Title. III. Title: Manuscrits du déluge. English.
PS8553.O7745M3513 2004   C842'.54   C2003-907297-5

The publisher gratefully acknowledges the financial support of the Canada Council for the Arts; the Government of Canada through the Book Publishing Industry Development Program; and the Province of British Columbia through the British Columbia Arts Council for our publishing activities.

  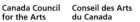

… for my parents and my friend Bill Glassco.

*"Foam, spill upon the bridge and over the woods;—
black palls and the organ's roll,—lightning and
thunder,—rise up and roll;—Waters and sorrows, rise
and lift high the Floods. For ever since they have
vanished—oh the precious gems burying themselves
and the full-blown flowers! What tedium it all is!"*

Arthur Rimbaud, *After the Flood*
Translated by Daniel Sloate

Written on Water was commissioned and developed by CanStage, Toronto, Canada and the Melbourne Festival, Melbourne, Australia.

The English-language premiere production of the play was produced by CanStage, Toronto and the National Arts Centre, Ottawa, Canada. *Written on Water* premiered in Toronto at the Bluma Appel Theatre, on January 22, 2004 and in Ottawa at the Theatre of the National Arts Centre, on February 26, 2004. The production was directed by Micheline Chévrier with the cast of Doris Chilcott, David Fox, Jerry Franken, Barbara Gordon, Carolyn Heatherington and Brian Marler.

The play premiered in French on February 13, 2003 in a version entitled *Les Manuscrits du déluge* at the Théâtre du Nouveau Monde, Lorraine Pintal, Artistic Director. The production was directed by Barbara Nativi, with the cast of Benoît Girard, Monique Mercure, Monique Miller, Gérard Poirier, Sébastien Ricard and Louise Turcot.

The French version entitled *Les Manuscrits du déluge* is published by Leméac Éditeur, Montreal. The Italian version entitled *I Manoscritti del Diluvo* is published by UBU LIBRI, Milano.

I want to thank the members of the group "J'écris ma vie 2000", from the Lac Saint-Jean Historical Society, who were, along with my parents, the true source of inspiration for this play. Thanks, too, to the Melbourne International Festival (2000) and CanStage in Toronto, for having initiated this project, with the support of the Canada Council for the Arts.

I would also like to thank the Australian and English Canadian and Québécois actors who participated in the various workshops in Melbourne (2000), in Toronto (2001) and Montreal (2002).

Many thanks to Linda Gaboriau, translator, David Latham, director, and Iris Turcott, dramaturge. My deep gratitude and affection to Louis Gravel for his unflagging support and his love.

—M.M.B

Memories and Floods...

The flood is a complex metaphor that represents the end of one world and the beginning of another.

The flood is a metaphor that represents the devastating waves of homogenization, social conformity and globalization that dictate our lives and serve to standardize specific cultures and make collective memories seem like suspect acts, even acts of terrorism.

The flood is the oppressive trend of "Young is beautiful", a trend where the elderly are seen as only fit to occupy territories prefabricated by men and women in suits.

In these troubled times when floods are unleashed every day, when our powerful and belligerent neighbour is prepared to resort to lies in order to extend its supremacy over the entire planet, our cultures and memories are like these characters, these seniors who are struggling against inevitable extinction.

One world is dying ... What will be the basis of the next?

I hope it is dignified.

—Michel Marc Bouchard

CAST OF CHARACTERS

DANNY-THE-LONELY-CHILD: A young man in his twenties. The only child who didn't leave the village.

CLAIRE: Widow, member of the writing circle. Martha's friend.

SAMUEL: Widower, Martha's brother. In charge of the writing circle.

DOROTHY: William's wife. Member of the writing circle.

WILLIAM: Dorothy's husband. Member of the writing circle.

MARTHA: Samuel's sister. Unmarried. Member of the writing circle.

SET

An old school gymnasium that has been converted into a writing room. Long reading tables float on the flooded floor. The windows are shattered. Thousands of pages of manuscripts are scattered everywhere. There is a large, damaged bookcase in the background.

All the characters, except Danny, are wearing identical rubber boots, courtesy of Public Security. The singer, Monica Bacio, is a figment of the author's imagination, as is her song.

Scene 1

DANNY-THE-LONELY-CHILD appears carrying a pair of wings that are tattered and splattered with mud.

DANNY
(*reading*)
"The rain poured down,
The rain poured down relentlessly,
The rained poured down relentlessly, without
cease.

"A river of rain
had been falling from the sky
all morning.

"In the middle of our dreams,
In the middle of the night,
A thunderclap.
It came from upstream.
A roll of drums.
Drums of war.

"Then came the wave of mud ...
I saw the North Bridge sail by ...
Like a ship at sea.
I saw the East Bridge sail by ...
Like a bird in the sky.

"The church lay down in the middle of the river.
The wings of an angel from a forgotten pageant
escaped. And not so far away, in our writing room,

the window cracks,shatters. Our manuscripts are swept away, thousands of pages. The torrent gushed reams of paper through the broken window ... Our pages."

The title: "Chronicle of the Flood."

Scene 2

CLAIRE

(*as she throws a dead cat in the air*)
If I throw him a bit higher, he'll have time to
realize what's happening to him. It'll give his
instinct a chance to revive. Cats always land on
their feet. Always. (*Beat.*) They can be hypocritical,
too. You call them and they don't come. You say:
Live! And they don't live. (*Beat.*) How am I going
to tell her? Good news, Martha. I found your cat.
Bad news. He isn't landing on his feet. Death is
the hardest truth to hide. And "*A half-truth is a
whole lie.*" *Reader's Digest.* (*Beat. She hugs the cat.*) I've
always been too nice. The right comment at the
right time, the perfect little compliment, the
dumb little smile. Too nice. All that grinning to
please others must've given me more than my
share of wrinkles. I'm sure that seventy years of
niceness have deformed my face. I bought a
Jacuzzi even though I knew that swirling water
would make me dizzy, just because I didn't want to
disappoint the salesman who'd come all the way to
our remote town. If you ask me, niceness is the
worst quality. I don't think it's a quality at all. It
makes you weak. (*Beat. She holds the cat tight.*) I'm
going to throw you up in the air one last time, and
as you fall, you're going to roll over and land on
your feet. (*She throws him up in the air.*) Roll over!
Roll over! (*It hits the ground with a thud.*) Nine lives,
eh? Well, I guess he's had his eight bonuses. (*She
stuffs the cat into her handbag.*) My title: "Martha's
Cat is Dead." (*The loud noise of a helicopter overhead.
She disappears.*)

Scene 3

SAMUEL is sorting soggy documents. DOROTHY and WILLIAM are giving him a hand. SAMUEL puts the texts by authors who have died in a pile and carefully files the work of living authors.

SAMUEL

"Christmas Holidays."

WILLIAM

Leopold Simon.

DOROTHY

Dead, two years ago.

SAMUEL

He won't be able to restore his manuscript.

WILLIAM

"The Municipal Elections."

DOROTHY

Anita Plourde.

WILLIAM

Cerebral embolism.

DOROTHY

Five years ago.

SAMUEL

Another manuscript lost. (*reading another text*) "For the occasion, the furniture store was full of people. Many had come from neighbouring towns. After some opening comments, the salesman solemnly turned the appliance on. It was breathtaking."

DOROTHY

That's "The Arrival of the First Colour TV" by Lucie Tremblay.

WILLIAM
Osteoporosis.

DOROTHY
No, that was her sister. She was colon cancer.

WILLIAM
(*reading*) "Waltzing to the rhythm of the waves, their graceful profile on the horizon … "

SAMUEL
"Ships Ahoy."

WILLIAM
By Louis Scott.

DOROTHY
Alive.

SAMUEL
Manuscript saved. "Golden Wedding Anniversary."

WILLIAM
Laurent Blackburn. Alzheimer's.

DOROTHY
Still alive.

WILLIAM
Somebody should tell him.

SAMUEL
Trout Fishing.

WILLIAM
(*he takes a sheet of paper out of his shirt pocket and reads*) "The experts say it's an 'incredibly rare' natural phenomenon. But I say it was predictable. With all the junk we've been feeding him for years now, something like this was to be expected. The garbage pails full of dead foetuses, the condoms full of living viruses. All the young people

committing suicide, and the old people who refuse to die. He couldn't keep all that inside anymore. It had to come out. A body has its limits. No wonder he seems to have been sitting tight for the past few years. He was getting ready. He made man in his image, and man does that sitting down. The clouds parted and all the excrement of the Supreme Being rained down on us. Thunderous farts. Furious lightning. Hours of divine defecation. An incredibly rare natural phenomenon." My title: "God's Incontinence." (*Beat.*)

SAMUEL
"History of the Choir" and "Mrs. Turcotte, Teacher and Singer."

WILLIAM
No comments on my new piece of writing?

DOROTHY
(*she reads a text she takes out of her handbag.*)
"A dress for eternity. When I saw the mudslide headed our way, that was all I could think of. A dress for eternity. Not an easy choice. You can easily make the worst mistake. One day someone says you look good in red, but in the final analysis, you should have worn blue all your life. Flowing sleeves. To allow for the position of the hands folded on the stomach. Filmy fabric for heaven and a brazen print for hell. A green dress is ridiculous. I don't want to die in green. I'll choose a classic black." My title: "A Black Dress for Eternity." (*Beat.*)

WILLIAM
Did you like what Dorothy wrote, Sam?

SAMUEL

"The First Day of School." That was mine.

WILLIAM

Don't you have anything to say about our compositions?

SAMUEL

(*distracted*) Very good. Very, very good.

WILLIAM

If you feel like criticizing them, go ahead … You were never shy.

SAMUEL

Well, you know me, divine defecation …

WILLIAM

Is that all you've got to say?

SAMUEL

… and dresses for burials.

> *Beat.*

DOROTHY

Is that all?

SAMUEL

(*annoyed*) I'm too worried about everything we have to save to be interested in your new material.

WILLIAM

Too worried! Too worried! If you filed them in alphabetical order, it would make things a lot easier.

SAMUEL

Alphabetical order!?! The Gagnons next to the Goulets—impossible! One day the Goulet boy stole old man Gagnon's car. And the Gagnons next to the Gauthiers won't work either. The Gagnons' son divorced the Gauthiers' daughter. The Goulets always felt very close to the Savards. The Savards had no time for the Simards who always had a lot of respect for the Blackburns. In order, that makes Goulet, Savard, Blackburn, Simard—

WILLIAM

I just thought alphabetical order would spare you all that trouble and you'd have more time to devote to our new work.

SAMUEL

"The Arrival of the Mini-Skirt."

DOROTHY

(*looking at the document*) That one was mine. "There seemed to be no end to the exposure of thighs." The water has erased the rest.

SAMUEL

Sit down and write the damaged parts out again.

DOROTHY

What?

SAMUEL

Take a clean sheet of paper, sit down and try to remember the missing passages. You're going to do it for every one of your texts.

DOROTHY

I don't know about the rest of you, but I intend to save what's left of my memory for things to come, not things of the past.

SAMUEL

(*he passes a document to DOROTHY and WILLIAM and recites*)
"Exodus of the Children."

"No more trees. They'd been clearing the forest for decades. No more trees to be cut.

The news struck, like an axe striking a sick old pine.

We were shattered.

The young people are leaving for the city.

The first ones leave ... the others follow close behind.

The noisy little bar where they gathered to remake the world falls silent.

The thickets that hid their first kisses are now overgrown.

The backyards are deserted and the school is empty ... "

Did I make any mistakes?

WILLIAM

No.

SAMUEL

Now we can reread everything we wrote. We're so lucky!

WILLIAM

Are you trying to tell us this flood is a piece of good luck?

DOROTHY

That's denial, Samuel! The flood psychologist talked about that. Denial. In the aftermath of catastrophes, victims look for the bright side of what they've been through. He says it's a matter of survival. Our lives are a shambles, and we refuse to see it. But very soon, it'll all come crashing down. He called it "the crash of the aftershock." He made it sound so serious.

SAMUEL

The flood psychologist?

DOROTHY

He's here to help us understand what we've just experienced.

SAMUEL

A meteorologist would've done the trick.

DOROTHY

He's a specialist in natural catastrophes and in the elderly.

WILLIAM

That must be the same branch.

SAMUEL

Any idea where the others are?

Silence.

DOROTHY

"There seemed to be no end to the exposure of thighs." That's all I can remember.

SAMUEL

William, you're going to restore your piece on "Small Game Hunting." The conclusion has disappeared.

WILLIAM

And what am I supposed to do?

SAMUEL

The conclusion.

WILLIAM

(*sarcastically*) "Three hares, two cases of beer and a headache." How's that for a conclusion?

SAMUEL

Sit down and pick up your pen.

WILLIAM

I won't sit down and I won't pick up my pen.

SAMUEL

You owe it to our chronicles.

WILLIAM

"Our chronicles! Our chronicles!" Fancy words!

SAMUEL

(*insisting*) Yes, our chronicles!

WILLIAM

Our harmless rambling.

SAMUEL

Don't you dare say that.

WILLIAM

A hobby for old folks.

SAMUEL

I forbid you.

WILLIAM

A pastime for amateurs.

SAMUEL

Individually, our pieces might not be important.
Perhaps they're just harmless ramblings, as you say,
but together, they mean something. Together
they're important. They constitute one small
society's view of society in general.

WILLIAM

(*to DOROTHY*) Does utopia come between denial
and the crash?

SAMUEL

(*impassioned*) It's our legacy to humanity.

DOROTHY

"The Arrival of the Mini-skirt"? A legacy to humanity?

SAMUEL

Nothing is more important than our writing.

WILLIAM

(*sarcastically*) The bridges are in the fields, the church is in the riverbed, our houses are piled on top of each other, but nothing is more important than our scraps of soggy paper!

SAMUEL

We can't allow the flood to decide what will disappear and what will remain of us.

WILLIAM

Maybe we have other plans, instead of rehashing all this.

DOROTHY

That's right, other plans.

SAMUEL

You can't really think that.

WILLIAM

Why shouldn't we think that ? We have a right to think what we think and a right to say it. There you go again, treating us like idiots. You have a right to disagree with what we think. That's your right. But we have a right to think what we think and to say it. And if we say we think we have other plans, it's because we must have other plans.

SAMUEL

I asked you to write what's missing in your texts and I have a right to ask you to write what's missing in your texts. There you go again, defying me. And if I tell you to write what's missing in your texts, it's because you're going to write what's missing in your texts.

Scene 4

DANNY

(*memorizing*) "The garbage pails full of living foetuses, condoms full of dead viruses ... " No, it's the other way around. "Dead foetuses, living viruses ... All the young people committing suicide, and the old people who refuse to die." Mr. Samuel refused to let me in again. I told him, everything's changed. The sky has fallen on the earth. Let me come in. Someday, I'm going to fly. If he lets me in, I'm going to fly. "All the young people committing suicide, and the old people who refuse to die." Mr. William suggested that they change the filing system. Mrs. Dorothy is going to rewrite the mini-skirt and Mr. William, small-game hunting. The flood psychologist says we're going to feel optimistic today. (*memorizing*) "One day, someone tells you you look good in red, but in the final analysis, you should have worn blue all your life."

Scene 5

DOROTHY

(*re-reading*) "The scrap of material called a mini-skirt was making our men nervous. Why were women undressing like this? Did this shocking exposure of their bottoms really help their cause?" Three sentences. All I could remember was three sentences ... and I'm not sure they're accurate.

SAMUEL

How about you, William?

WILLIAM

(*his arms crossed*) I'm busy thinking and I have a right to be busy thinking.

DOROTHY

(*She tears up the sheet of paper and starts over.*) "I was the first one to wear a mini-skirt. I had the nicest legs in town. Long and beautiful. I was the first one to go out dressed like that, showing off all my assets."

SAMUEL

May I ask what you're doing?

DOROTHY

What?

SAMUEL

What's that supposed to be?

DOROTHY

I'm redoing my piece.

SAMUEL

That's called rewriting.

DOROTHY

    Call it whatever you want.

SAMUEL

    You can't rewrite your past.

DOROTHY

    I just did ... and actually, it's a lot easier than I thought.

SAMUEL

    You can't do that.

DOROTHY

    What's the point of rewriting your life if you can't correct a few bits?

SAMUEL

    The past is absolute. It can't be altered.

DOROTHY

    I don't want eternity to remember me as being uptight.

SAMUEL

    Well, you were.

WILLIAM

    That's my wife you're speaking to.

SAMUEL

    You're supposed to be off hunting.

    CLAIRE enters, carrying her handbag under her arm.

CLAIRE

    (*picking up on the prevailing tension*) I brought some survival bars. Fruit and nuts. I got them in the relief tent. The Public Security people say it's important to eat during a crisis. It lowers the tension. I've already had three of them. Still can't feel the effect. Morning, William. Your hair looks very, very pretty, Dorothy. It makes you look younger.

DOROTHY
That's the point, isn't it?

WILLIAM
It's all natural hair. They call them "extensions."

CLAIRE
I finally got to see your new living room set.

DOROTHY
Where?

CLAIRE
The sofa was in a ditch, the armchair outside the grocery store.

DOROTHY
And our china cabinet?

CLAIRE
No sign of it.

DOROTHY
A halogen light with a red base?

CLAIRE
All that must've looked nice together.

SAMUEL
You're late, Claire.

CLAIRE
"*Punctuality is the art of waiting for others.*" I found that in *Let's Laugh.* They were interviewing me again.

SAMUEL

Ever since they arrived with their truck with the big antenna, they've been looking for blood.

CLAIRE

Is that what those big antennas are for?

SAMUEL

A figure of speech.

CLAIRE

Another figure of speech?! I can't keep up with them.

SAMUEL

Ever since they found Stanislas's widow's body floating downstream, we've graduated from a "natural disaster" to a "national tragedy." Stanislas's widow has become a national tragedy. I never would've thought she had such potential.

CLAIRE

That's not nice.

SAMUEL

When her kids left, she refused to join our group.

DOROTHÉE

They found her clinging to a beam from her house … completely nude. Do you realize what it means to be completely nude at our age?

CLAIRE

"Time is a stranger who settles inside us."

WILLIAM

Where did you get that one?

CLAIRE

House and Garden.

DOROTHÉE

She was completely nude, in front of dozens of curious onlookers. We all deserve to die with dignity, and at our age, dignity is fully dressed.

CLAIRE

"Death is the only competition where everyone wants to arrive last." The Farmer's Almanac.

SAMUEL

She was in charge of the pottery club. Really, a hopeless case.

WILLIAM

It's a great loss.

SAMUEL

Yes, a great loss for terracotta lovers.

WILLIAM

Who cares if it's writing or pottery, if it helps us pass the time—

SAMUEL

You can't refer to our work here as a pastime. Did anyone see the others headed this way?

CLAIRE

Did you hear they're going to dynamite the church? It's blocked the river. They're going to put explosives in the alcoves where the saints used to be. But first, they're going to ring the bell one last time.

SAMUEL

"The Arrival of the First Microwave." That was yours, Claire.

CLAIRE

"How did this mysterious, invisible force cook our food?"

DOROTHY

Sam wants us to rewrite our lives.

CLAIRE

Rewrite our lives?

SAMUEL

That's not what I said.

WILLIAM

(*reading what he has just written*) "In conclusion, the most wonderful thing about small-game hunting is that there's nobody around to tell you what you should do, what you should say, and least of all, what you should think."

SAMUEL

You never wrote that.

WILLIAM

It's my new conclusion.

CLAIRE

If I could rewrite my life, today I would've arrived before everyone else, just so the two of us could be alone together, Samuel ... even though I've never known how to be alone together with you. I'm easily intimidated, so talking to you, alone together ... You've always acted like a teacher, knowing, never doubting how things should be and how things should be done. When our children left, you saved us from sadness by turning the school gymnasium into a writing room. Even though it felt strange to be sitting in front of you like our kids before us, even though it wasn't always easy to write stories that seemed unimportant, we followed you. The more we wrote, the more writing seemed to make everything "precious." That was your word, "precious." You had us doing all sorts of grand things. Allegories, metaphors, figures of speech. If I could rewrite my life, I'd find the courage to tell you that this flood of ours isn't so awful. A village where you never hear a thing, a mute village where you never hear a child laugh, isn't normal. There was too much silence. Too much silence isn't good. It's like a foretaste of death. And God takes advantage of it. Silence encourages Him to talk to us all the time. I just walked by what's left of my house. I should have felt sad like everyone else. Ruins are all that's left of my life with my dear deceased, and that's just fine. If I could rewrite my life, I'd tell you, without trembling, that I've read the brochures the men from the city, in their suits and ties, have been distributing to the victims of the flood. They have very nice customized apartments to offer. If I could live my life over again, I'd tell you I want to go live there. (*She is having trouble breathing. Beat.*) I never asked anybody for anything. I never asked for a Jacuzzi and I have one. I never asked for a husband and I had one. It's not easy for me to think about myself for once. (*Beat.*) If I could rewrite my life, I'd tell you: Samuel, I want to leave with your sister. I want to go live in the city with Martha. You know how much I care about her. No, you don't know … I haven't told her about my plan yet. If your sister decides to come with me, I'm asking you not to interfere. I'd say all that to you. Then, I'd raise my eyes to the heavens and I'd say: may Stanislas's widow forgive me, but this flood is really extraordinary.

SAMUEL

And what would your title be?

CLAIRE

There wouldn't be a title.

SAMUEL

A story without a title?

CLAIRE

It wouldn't be a story. It would be a wish.

SAMUEL

And how would I answer in your wish without a title?

CLAIRE

Positively.

SAMUEL

You don't know me very well.

MARTHA enters the writing room.

MARTHA

(*holding a sheet of paper*) "Return of the Young People." That's my title. "Martha was delighted by the arrival of all the young volunteers. She watched the tall, virile teenagers working to raze the only wall left standing from our poor church. Bare-chested, dressed in yellow slicker pants. The sweat of exertion gleaming on their faces, their thick locks swaying in the wind like a field of golden wheat. Their firm muscles, tensed and indecent. She, who never kneels, kneeled. 'O Lord, let the wall resist and let the show go on and on.' At nightfall, in the relief tent, the courting ritual began. The conquests of a single glance, a brush of the hand, an unfinished sentence, a stifled laugh, a bracelet exchanged like an eternal vow. And the rustling of clothes slipping; youthful valleys and tight, smooth bellies with downy hair, round bums like ripe fruits, firm breasts pointing like exclamation marks, tongues bespeaking pleasure ... Promising bulges in white underwear ... And the candles wavering in the wind. Bums, breasts, tongues, saliva, vagina, phallus, clitoris—"

SAMUEL

(*He takes* MARTHA'*s sheet of paper and continues reading.*) "Martha's hand, so well-behaved for so long, caressed her body, farther and farther down ... " Is that your piece on the flood?

MARTHA

I haven't finished.

CLAIRE

Well, I think it's very daring. I think it's very unusual.

SAMUEL

(*violently*) Well, I think nobody asked you what you thought.

> *Long silence. Uneasiness.*

MARTHA

(*to break the silence*) They say there are two hundred young volunteers.

WILLIAM

For seventy-two inhabitants. That makes three each.

SAMUEL

And I saw one boy in a skirt. This isn't Scotland, last I heard.

MARTHA

Their freedom is so extraordinary.

SAMUEL

(*cynically*) Extraordinary! They wear skirts! Extraordinary! Harmless young people who'll do everything to make us feel attached to them, and then they'll take off and abandon us. Don't you remember what we went through?

MARTHA

It's not the same.

SAMUEL

You never had any children, so be quiet.

CLAIRE

(*coming to* MARTHA*'s defense*) *"The elderly have to be handled with care, like wilted roses that lose their petals at the slightest touch."*

SAMUEL

Do you all enjoy seeing our writing room in this state?

CLAIRE

"Laughter is a speck of joy that makes the brain sneeze."

SAMUEL

Claire, have another survival bar. Maybe you only begin to feel the effect after four. (*to* MARTHA, *exploding*) At our age, we should cultivate elegance to compensate for appearance! Vulgarity might be charming in young people, but in us it's disgraceful.

MARTHA

I'm going to ask my young volunteer with the sink stopper ring through her eyebrow to help me put my clothesline back up. I'm going to hang our archives out to dry. Hundreds of loads of hundreds of pages. We'll let our colours fly.

DOROTHY

What kind of a ring does she have where?

MARTHA

A metal ring through her eyebrow.

CLAIRE

Through her eyebrow?

MARTHA

I'd seen it on television before, but in person, it's much more impressive.

CLAIRE

Is it something medical?

WILLIAM

It's called "body piercing."

DOROTHY

Body what?

MARTHA

Piercing.

WILLIAM

Some women even have them on their nipples.

CLAIRE

I suppose that's a figure of speech, too?

DOROTHY

What's it for?

WILLIAM

It's supposed to be decorative.

DOROTHY
Who told you that?

WILLIAM
One of the male volunteers.

DOROTHY
There are things people should keep to themselves.

WILLIAM
Don't act so prim and proper. Tell them you like it when your man makes love to you twice in a row.

DOROTHY
That's right—once in the winter, once in the summer. (*Laughter.*)

SAMUEL
Have you finished acting like a bunch of kids? And where is everyone else? Do you know what's keeping them?

Beat.

MARTHA
(*gravely*) They're not coming, Sam.

SAMUEL
What?

MARTHA
The others won't be coming anymore.

SAMUEL
Why?

MARTHA
Because that's how it is.

SAMUEL
That can't be how it is.

MARTHA
That's how it is.

SAMUEL
They can't … (*Beat.*) What reason can …

WILLIAM
With everything that's happened, you have to understand that some people…

MARTHA
(*to* SAM) You should sit down.

SAMUEL
The Gravels? The Blackburns?

MARTHA
No.

      Beat.

SAMUEL
What will we do about their manuscripts?

WILLIAM
(WILLIAM *takes a brochure out of his pocket.*) "The Gateway to Paradise. The doors open automatically thanks to an electronic eye. A security system guarantees the residents' safety. Meals, prepared to meet specific dietary needs, are served at set times. The bathrooms—"

MARTHA
You're leaving, too?

DOROTHY
We'll be living on the twelfth floor.

WILLIAM
A great view of the city.

DOROTHY

A beautiful choice of wallpaper. And they even have a dentist on call.

WILLIAM

She wants to have crowns planted.

DOROTHY

That's not what they call it—

WILLIAM

A screwed-in smile, is that better?

Heavy silence.

DOROTHY

(*DOROTHY hands a document to SAMUEL.*) These are the papers for the compensation on our duplex. Since you're co-owner with us … You know, the money they give to victims—

SAMUEL

(*bitterly*) You want to know where your beautiful natural hair comes from? It was stolen from a little Latin American girl while she was sound asleep. Her mother betrayed her and sold her beautiful hair to some vultures who resold it at an outrageous price so some old bag can go on believing she's eternal.

DOROTHY

Why are you insulting me?

SAMUEL

Wearing hair stolen from a child, is that your eternity?

DOROTHY

Why is he insulting me?

WILLIAM

We're moving to be closer to our children!

SAMUEL

Go ahead. Go live near your ungrateful offspring.
You'll be able to gauge the extent of their
selfishness.

DOROTHY

What makes you say dreadful things like that?

MARTHA

(*trying to reason with him*) Wish them well, Samuel.

SAMUEL

Blood of your blood. Flesh of your flesh. What's
left for you of this meat gone to rot far away, from
their parents?

MARTHA

Wish them well.

SAMUEL

What's left of our children for us? A phone call on
our birthdays? Falling sick to force them to visit?
The unnerving resemblance when they're around?
The boring family get-togethers that drag on? You
call that, our children? My title: "Traces of
Children"!! Do you really think that by going to
live near them, you'll make up for lost time?
They're emotion addicts who operate on guilt
when it comes to us. Egotists who can hardly wait
to impress their dinner guests by describing how
they were finally there, when we drew our last
breath, how they finally held us in their arms, how
they finally told us that they loved us. In their
disposable world, we old people are at the bottom

of the barrel. Not one of them has ever come to read our work. Not a single one!

WILLIAM

We should've left with them, instead of spending our time writing about the past.

SAMUEL

That's not what you really think!?

WILLIAM

(*shouting*) That's what I really think and I've got a right to think what I want!

CLAIRE

(*to SAMUEL*) At least take a look at the brochure. Just a peek. Look at the woman, she's wearing a beautiful string of pearls. Her husband is serving her a cup of tea. They're smiling at each other. He smiles without showing his teeth. It's more masculine. I don't understand the woman's eyes. She's not looking at the man or the cup. It looks like they redrew her eyes. Maybe she was sick? But they don't put sick old ladies in beautiful ads. (*handing the brochure to SAMUEL*) Look, Sam. It's so colourful and everyone's smiling.

SAMUEL

Colourful! Customized prisons with spectacular views of the highway. Colourful! I have my title for the week: "The Colourful Exodus of the Elderly." (*improvising*) "The elderly were kept in six-by-six foot pens! The elderly were given big beds equipped with genuine leather straps to restrain the runaways! The elderly kept themselves busy, contemplating the ceiling, counting their pills and perpetually waiting for visitors. The elderly with

the elderly, watching each other grow old. The
Gateway to Paradise and everyone is smiling!"

WILLIAM

It's more luxurious than you think.

SAMUEL

"Luxurious" in their jargon means you get more
than one bath a week.

DOROTHY

You gave us a lot, Samuel—

SAMUEL

Save your gratitude for your hairdresser.

MARTHA

(*to SAM*) I think we should cancel today's meeting.

SAMUEL

And when will you be leaving me?

MARTHA

Me?

SAMUEL

It's true, you haven't heard Claire's proposal yet.

MARTHA

What proposal?

CLAIRE

You can't tell her that.

SAMUEL

Sorry, I forgot I'm not supposed to intervene.

MARTHA

What are you talking about?

SAMUEL

Right, Claire? I should keep my mouth shut?

CLAIRE
    I don't want it to happen like this!

MARTHA
    Claire, what is he talking about?

CLAIRE
    Not like this!

MARTHA
    Do you want to leave, too?

SAMUEL
    Tell her!

CLAIRE
    I have nothing to tell her.

SAMUEL
    Come on! Let the cat out of the bag!

        Beat.

CLAIRE
    (*upset*) How did you know? How did you know he
    was in there?

SAMUEL
    Go ahead! Make your proposal.

CLAIRE
    Nobody knows.

SAMUEL
    I promise not to intervene.

CLAIRE
    Nobody knows.

MARTHA
    You told Samuel you wanted to leave with me?

CLAIRE
    You can't know what's in my bag!

MARTHA
Look at me, Claire.

CLAIRE
(*trying to calm herself down*) I'll bring you all some more survival bars. We'll go looking for your halogen lamp, Dorothy. Your hair looks very nice.

DOROTHY
A little Latin American girl says thanks.

CLAIRE
(*so upset she's almost incoherent*) "Anger … Anger is an avalanche that crushes … " No. "Anger is an avalanche that … Anger … crushes … an avalanche that crushes everything … " No. "On everything it crushes." That's it. *"Anger is an avalanche that crumbles on everything it crushes."*

CLAIRE exits with her handbag.

WILLIAM
Sign the papers, Sam.

SAMUEL
No twelfth floor with wallpaper? Forced to rewrite everything before Sam will sign?

DOROTHY
Let's go, William.

SAMUEL
Follow her, William. "Shadow of His Old Lady!" How's that for a title?

WILLIAM
Today I understand why your wife died of sorrow.

SAMUEL
You have no right.

WILLIAM

And you have every right?

SAMUEL

You'll end up helpless, useless. Incapable of
rebuilding your houses, incapable of fighting to
defend your life's work. I'll write about your
departure the way one writes about great defeats.
I'll denounce you the way one denounces cowards.
I'll re-file you all. I'll rewrite everything. Until my
eyesight fails, until my aching hands can no longer
hold a pen, until my memory becomes a blur. I'll
rework my manuscript and, among the things the
flood took from me, I'll add your names. Go
pursue your grand plans! Go get your screw-in
dentures.

The sound of the church bells tolling.

WILLIAM

Do you hear that, Sam? Your world has passed
away.

WILLIAM and DOROTHY exit.

MARTHA

You really handled the meeting well! "Shadow of
His Old Lady!" "Old bag!" You found words to
please everyone.

SAMUEL

Aren't you going to run after them and apologize
for having such a monster for a brother?

MARTHA

Why run?

SAMUEL

Go tell them they've forgotten the meaning of
pride. Go tell them—

MARTHA

Step down from your pulpit! It's just the two of us.

SAMUEL

"And Martha's hand caressing ... " How do you explain this libidinous resurrection?

MARTHA

I mustn't forget my appointment with my young volunteer. She had her first orgasm at thirteen. She promised she'd tell me about it. Come here, let me straighten your shirt collar.

SAMUEL

Keep your awkward gestures to yourself. (*Despite this, she fixes his collar. She runs her fingers through his hair.*) Leave my hair alone! They've all surrendered to "fate." The word of the weak and inferior.

MARTHA

Look how you put your belt on. Raise your arms so I can fix your belt. Take off your shoes so I can pull up your socks. Your shoes. The other shoe.

SAMUEL

(*crushed*) What use am I if they leave? What use am I if you leave?

MARTHA

What?

SAMUEL

If you leave with Claire?

MARTHA

I'll go where you go. If you decide to stay, I'll stay. If you want us to write everything again, we'll write everything again. If you want to yell at me, you'll yell at me. I'll go where you go, Sam.

Scene 6

The church bells toll.

DANNY

> (*Standing, wearing his wings, he is memorizing* MARTHA's *text.*) "She stopped to say a brief prayer. She, who never kneels, kneeled. 'O Lord, let the wall resist and let the show go on and on.' (*The dull thud of an explosion.* DANNY *crosses himself and recites:*) Saliva, vagina, phallus, clitoris … "

Scene 7

CLAIRE

(*patting her handbag*) "*Let the cat out of the bag: a
figure of speech meaning: reveal a concealed truth.*"
Another figure of speech I didn't expect. I can't
keep up with them. My speciality is maxims, not
figures of speech. We have to start all over again.
Like yesterday, when they dragged me out of the
mud, they all thought I was dead until I screamed.
When I saw the sun, I wondered why I was still
here, why all this violence if we were not meant to
die? (*Beat.*) She'll never understand why I waited
so long to tell her. If I were a good author, I'd
know how to begin. By my desire to leave with her
or the news that her cat is dead. I would've found
the right words. All I know how to do is learn
stupid maxims and try to catch up with figures of
speech. My title: "Letting the Cat out of the Bag."

Scene 8

SAMUEL

>(*re-reading a damaged text*)
>"A woman lay on a veranda taking a rest
>Dozing, one shoulder bared
>The breeze, like a lover, revealed her breast
>
>"Hand on her forehead,
>Not fretting, dreaming instead,
>A picture of delight,
>Beyond anger or fright
>
>"My wife lay on the veranda taking a rest
>And I stood watching ... "
>
>No. That's not it.
>
>"My wife lay on the veranda taking a rest
>And I stood watching her ... "
>
>No ... I don't think there was any "her."

DANNY

>(*voice off*)
>"Like the breeze before me
>I lay down at her side
>Whispering, glad to be
>With my beautiful bride."

SAMUEL AND DANNY

>(*DANNY's voice off*)
>"A woman on the veranda taking no heed
>For a moment of bliss
>The man was freed
>From memories of all amiss
>For a moment of bliss."

SAMUEL

>You can come in. Today, you can come in.

DANNY

    (*enters wearing his wings*) "Danny-the-lonely-child, entered the big writing room. For ages he'd been wondering how he'd make his entrance in that place forbidden to those who'd never taken pen in hand there. It is a solemn occasion. His heart is beating fast. Danny-the-lonely-child, who talks alone, who walks alone, enters the writing room where time stands still. How will he tell his story? How will he begin?" A title. Let's give a title. Any title. "Danny-the-lonely-child, like a winged guardian, enters the writing room." Too long. "Like a winged guardian ... " It's a metaphor. The master says that a metaphor means using one image to describe another. "Danny and the Writing Room." That's my title. In our village, when someone announces a title, people listen.

SAMUEL

    I'm listening. Go on. (*DANNY falls silent, surprised by SAMUEL's gentle tone.*) Go on, I said.

DANNY

    "Danny-the-lonely-child, whose parents raised him on the Bible and prayers, enters the mysterious room. What should he say? What tale should he tell? He is intimidated."

SAMUEL

    Begin at the beginning.

DANNY

    "They say he's a holy man."

SAMUEL

    Why?

DANNY

    That's my title, "Danny, The Holy Man."

SAMUEL

    Go on.

DANNY

    "When the old priest died, Danny's parents were granted permission to give holy communion. Every Sunday, before sunrise, Danny stood at the roadside waiting for the bus that brought the consecrated hosts from the city. One day, he ate a whole box of them. And that is how he became a holy man."

SAMUEL

    Too short.

DANNY

    I'll never be good at this. No, don't use the future tense—

SAMUEL

    What does a host taste like?

DANNY

    I'm not used to your voice speaking so gently to me.

SAMUEL

    What does it taste like?

DANNY

    Christ in all his glory, suffering on the cross.

SAMUEL

    Is that all?

DANNY

    Some days, it tastes of Christ suffering, other days, it tastes of Christ in all his glory.

SAMUEL

    A good beginning.

DANNY
Why are you being so gentle?

SAMUEL
Take your time.

DANNY
Why aren't you kicking me out?

SAMUEL
Concentrate on your subject.

DANNY
Why aren't you pushing me aside?

SAMUEL
It's all jumbled.

DANNY
I won't leave!

SAMUEL
Spoken words are imperfect.

DANNY
I won't leave!

SAMUEL
We spend our lives correcting them.

DANNY
I'll stay, even if you yell at me.

SAMUEL
In writing, things can be set in order—

DANNY
Why aren't you saying mean things to me?

SAMUEL
You reduced your story about the hosts to three sentences. Put some mystery into it.

DANNY

I was prepared to defend myself. I would've answered: "Samuel! No, don't hit me! Let go of my arm. Stop. You've broken my wrist. You've broken my wrist!"

SAMUEL

How do you know about that?

DANNY

"That scrap of fabric, that's what they should have called the mini-skirt, made the men nervous." I also know: "In conclusion, when setting his traps, the trapper should never forget that animals have an advantage over us: their sense of smell. The hunter should avoid artificial scents. Avoid all soaps, perfumes, and especially the smell of gas."

SAMUEL

How do you do it?

DANNY

And this one: "How did this invisible, mysterious force cook food? It produced tidbits of cancer and women who ate microwaves would give birth to deformed creatures."

SAMUEL

How can you know all that?

DANNY

I know all the stories.

SAMUEL

I'm going to get some paper in the relief tent.

DANNY

In "Exodus of the Children," you forgot two sentences: "No more car races down the main street, no more swimming competitions in the river." Why did you let me in? Why today?

SAMUEL

I feel alone and a bit desperate. Is that a good enough answer?

DANNY

You should've put a bit of mystery into it.

SAMUEL

I'm the one who makes jokes around here.

DANNY

Okay.

SAMUEL

(*more formally*) There are rules.

DANNY

You're the president of the group. No one arrives late. Everyone has to respect the filing system. You're the only one to make jokes—

SAMUEL

My wife's broken arm ... that was an accident.

DANNY

We can't correct what she wrote. We don't have the right.

SAMUEL

You're right. We don't have the right.

DANNY

Today I entered the writing room. I'm happy.

SAMUEL

I'll bring back some paper. Boxes of paper.

> *SAMUEL exits.*

DANNY

> (*alone*) I'm going to sit where the others used to sit. I'll be Mrs. Claire, Mr. William and his wife, and all the others.

Scene 9

DOROTHY is holding a badly damaged halogen lamp with a red base and WILLIAM is trying to figure out how a cell phone works. Beat. DOROTHY pats her hair and improvises a text, without writing it.

DOROTHY

"Still enthralled by her mother's caresses in the night, and by the sound of scissors, the little South American girl opened her eyes and ran to the mirror. She couldn't believe it. She was delighted." (*imitating a Spanish accent*) "Mamá, Mamá! What a good job you did, Mamá! My hair is so short and shiny. That woman who lives far away is going to be so happy. Chignons and braids … every time she fixes her hair, she'll think of me. And I'm proud to do so much good with such a small gift." My title: "Curls of Happiness."

WILLIAM

(*holding a cell phone*) Did you see what they're giving out at the relief tent?

DOROTHY

A cell phone.

WILLIAM

When there's a cord, the conversation travels through the cord, but now, where does it go?

DOROTHY

What do you mean?

WILLIAM

Where does the conversation go when there's no cord?

DOROTHY

The airwaves travel.

WILLIAM

When I talk, I say words, not airwaves.

DOROTHY

The words are converted into airwaves. When they reach the house of the person whose number you've dialled, they're converted back into words.

WILLIAM

Stop talking to me like I was retarded.

DOROTHY

I'm not talking to you like you were retarded.

WILLIAM

When children ask questions, it's cute. But old people—

DOROTHY

You're not old.

WILLIAM

Not old! The things you have to listen to. Old is all I am. Could we stop being optimistic for a couple of minutes? Could we enter your "crash of the aftershock"? Not old. Being old is all I do, full-time now. I spit old age, I cough old age, I burp old age, I fart old age. Old age is coming out of every part of my body, at least, all the parts that are still working. Not old. I have a dozen jars of pills that greet me every morning: "Hello, we're here to remind you that you're old and if you manage to forget it during the day, we'll remind you again at night." Not old! The food in my dinner plate and the face in my mirror have become my worst enemies. Not old?!

DOROTHY

Well, I still feel young.

WILLIAM

Do you want to know—

DOROTHY

No, I don't want to know! Go find someone else to listen to your woes. I want to hear beautiful things. And yelling at me isn't going to solve our problems with Sam. Find a sheet of paper and write your text on small-game hunting. I'm sure he'll appreciate the gesture and sign the documents.

WILLIAM

I'd rather die than do what he wants.

DOROTHY

You're both stubborn old goats!

WILLIAM

(*dialling a number*) Hello … I don't know who I want to talk to. I just dialled any number … My wife told me I should talk to someone … Could you put an old man on the phone? … Well, find one. They're not hard to find, apparently there are more and more of us … What do you mean, age is relative … It is not relative. That's stupid advertising for women … Age is something very precise, sir, and it brings its share of precise problems. At fifteen, it's what to do with your sperm. At twenty, it's what to do with your feelings. At thirty, what to do with your money. At forty, what to do with your wife. At fifty, it's what to do with your hair. At sixty, it's what to do with your time. At seventy and up, it's what to do, period. I

need to talk to an ordinary old man who hasn't
been through a flood ... Is that too much to ask?

Scene 10

CLAIRE and MARTHA are sitting on a table looking toward the river.

CLAIRE

Are you sure this is the right place?

MARTHA

That's what my pierced volunteer told me.

CLAIRE

Someone's coming.

MARTHA

This will take our mind off things.

CLAIRE

Are we really going to see the volunteers naked?

MARTHA

She said at least twenty of them.

CLAIRE

I've never seen naked volunteers.

MARTHA

Bums, breasts, bellies...

CLAIRE

"Naked love warms body and soul." Ladies Home Journal.

MARTHA

There they are!

CLAIRE

Look how beautiful they are.

MARTHA

(*improvising*) "A great night. A great light in the middle of the night."

CLAIRE

"Dazzling, magical."

MARTHA

"Young women with skin so milky white."

CLAIRE

"Young men with skin of bronze."

MARTHA

"New life on the ruins of another era."

CLAIRE

"The earth brings forth another harvest."

MARTHA

"Hope."

CLAIRE

(*looking at* MARTHA *intensely*) Look they're kissing.

MARTHA

Yes, they're kissing. I can hardly wait to spruce myself up.

CLAIRE

You look beautiful, even when your hair's uncombed.

MARTHA

Those chemical toilets don't make you want to linger in front of the mirror.

CLAIRE

Some celebrities wanted to organise a telethon but apparently we don't have enough casualties. It's too bad. About the show, I mean. Maybe Monica Bacio would've participated. Have you had time to rehearse your dance steps? (*She starts humming.*)

"La luna / nel cielo resplende"
(*The moon in the sky so bright*)

"E di bianco / la notte accende"
(*Its glow lights up the night*)
"Cela al vicino / I nostri amori"
(*Cherishing the words of love we say*)
"Che poi all'alba / disertano î cuori"
(*Words that vanish with the break of day*)

MARTHA

Aren't you going to ask me about Max?

CLAIRE

It's true, I never ask about your cat. I guess I
should. Have you found Max yet?

MARTHA

No sign of him, no matter how much I call.

CLAIRE

Maybe he can't hear you anymore.

MARTHA

You should tell me not to worry, he'll show up.

CLAIRE

You're right. I should say that. Don't worry. He'll
show up. (*Beat.*) You know, the night of the flood,
I was worried about you. When I saw the mud
carry away my kitchen, I prayed that you were safe.
I felt so bad about the fight we had the day before.

MARTHA

What did we fight about?

CLAIRE

Max and my asthma.

MARTHA

As usual.

CLAIRE

(*holding a letter*) I wrote something for you.

MARTHA

(*touched*) You wrote to me?

CLAIRE

(*handing her the letter*) You don't have to read it right away, right away.

MARTHA

It's for when I'm alone?

CLAIRE

That's right. When you're alone. (*Beat.*)

MARTHA

If someone told me, Max is dead, I'd hate that person till my dying day.

CLAIRE

Even if that person had nothing to do with your cat's death?

MARTHA

A bearer of bad tidings. Who'd want to hurt me like that? A real monster.

CLAIRE

(*taking back her letter*) I'll give it back to you later. It could use more figures of speech.

MARTHA

You wrote me sweet nothings?

CLAIRE

(*lying*) That's right.

MARTHA

Give me your hands. Your beautiful hands, full of memories. (*She takes CLAIRE's hands in hers.*)

CLAIRE

(*touched by MARTHA's gesture*) My daughter will be here tomorrow.

MARTHA

So soon?

CLAIRE

We're going to visit the customized apartments. One room should be enough.

MARTHA

One room isn't a home.

CLAIRE

Our world grows smaller as we grow older.

MARTHA

Where did you find that?

CLAIRE

Nowhere. Sometimes I have thoughts of my own.

MARTHA

(*kissing her hands*) Your soft hands.

CLAIRE

She'll take me shopping. Whenever my daughter doesn't know what to do with me, she takes me shopping.

MARTHA

She has a credit card instead of a personality.

CLAIRE

You have your brother.

MARTHA

(*with a trace of resignation*) You can't abandon your family.

CLAIRE

I suppose this is how things are meant to be.

MARTHA

I suppose.

Beat.

CLAIRE

If I asked you to come with me—

MARTHA

I've got my brother.

CLAIRE

I can see the two of us getting ready to leave.

MARTHA

Shhh.

CLAIRE

Just imagine all the crazy things we could do—

MARTHA

Never come back. Don't call me. Don't write. If you ever die, promise me you won't suffer.

CLAIRE

Wipe your tears.

MARTHA

What did you do with the rings from your dear deceased?

CLAIRE

I left them on my kitchen table the night of the flood.

MARTHA

You've lost your rings, I've lost my cat. Now we have nothing to fight about. (*moved*) I guess it's time for us to separate. (*taking a slip of paper out of her pocket*) "*Coals burn when they're close together, they die down when they're separated.*" I found it in a Chinese fortune cookie. I hoped there'd never be an occasion to give it to you. (*A moment of emotion.*)

CLAIRE

One last time? (*They kiss.*) Shall we join them?

> *MARTHA takes off her scarf. CLAIRE imitates her.*
> *They begin to undress. The loud sound of the*
> *helicopter overhead.*

Scene 11

DOROTHY

(*dressed in nightclothes that betray the figure of an old woman*) Some images are crueller than others. I wanted to surprise William. I went to ask the young volunteers to help me. There was a blank silence, harsher than any insults. I saw it in their eyes. "Too old." Their eyes shouted: "Too old." In their silence, I heard it all: "Breasts like saddle-bags, ass like a barn door, underarms like sheets on the line, belly of a beached whale, neck like a rooster's wattle, dentures of a skull, milky eyes, scaly nails, liver-spotted skin, mouth like a hen's ass." Their faces are wrinkle-free. Nothing written on their foreheads. Fattened on hormones, like plump flesh from the meat counter. Silly tattoos instead of personalities. I held back my tears and I said: Did you hear what I asked? Another silence, as if they wanted to finish me off. A bland blonde looked me over, from head to toe, smiling like a nurse about to unplug all the machines, and silently she shouted: "Too old." Would you rather see me old and weak, in my slippers knitting slippers? I just wanted my William to find me attractive. When he talked about it today, I realized that he'd like it. That's when I decided to go see the young people. (*Beat.*) Nowadays they can put titanium bolts in our mouths, nickel screws in our hips and metal bars in our legs. So is this too much to ask? My title: "A Little Ring." I want it on my left breast. Next to my heart.

She exits.

Scene 12

DANNY hands his assignments to SAMUEL.

DANNY

I've finished a fourth piece by the late Leopold Simon.

SAMUEL

Four!

DANNY

He was an easy writer to remember. He only used the verbs *to be* and *to have* and he found everything awful. I also have six pieces by the late Anita Plourde. She was the specialist in gossip and the word "unbelievable." And here are four more by the Tremblay sisters, experts in matters of the heart and the word "tears," queens of the expression: "He didn't deserve any better."

SAMUEL

I'm impressed.

DANNY

I remember. That's all.

SAMUEL

You could do Laurent Blackburn's piece on the golden wedding anniversary—

DANNY

Master of lists—the complete guest list for every event. One of the most difficult authors to memorize.

SAMUEL

Can you restore it?

DANNY
Right now?

SAMUEL
And Vivian Maltais's as well.

DANNY
"La Maltais." Poetry or literary dyslexia? We'll
never know. She'd always write *usurpate* instead of
usurp, she'd confuse *annals* and *anal* ... And
there's Mrs. Claire, our collector of maxims. And
Mr. William, king of details. Mrs. Dorothy and her
beautiful images. Mrs. Martha, the rebel ... I'm
tired.

SAMUEL
That's understandable. You're young.

DANNY
What?

SAMUEL
It was a joke.

DANNY
I could laugh, if you want.

SAMUEL
(*tenderly*) A while ago, I caught myself watching
you. Your enthusiasm for your work, your
concentration. I saw a bit of myself in you. There. I
said it.

DANNY
Is that true, what you just said?

SAMUEL
I told you once. I'll never say it again.

> Suddenly DANNY *takes him in his arms and lifts*
> *him off the ground.*

DANNY
I'm so happy.

SAMUEL
What are you doing?

DANNY
It's a sign of affection.

SAMUEL
You're holding me too tight.

DANNY
Just a bit longer.

SAMUEL
You're going to crush me.

> *MARTHA enters. She sees* SAMUEL *hitting* DANNY *so he'll put him down.*

MARTHA
Danny! Let him go! Let him go!

DANNY
It's not what you think.

MARTHA
Did he insult you?

DANNY
No.

MARTHA
What are you doing?

SAMUEL
It's a sign of affection.

MARTHA
Of what? For whom?

SAMUEL
For me.

MARTHA

A sign of what? For you?

DANNY

(*smiling*) Mrs. Martha is better at jokes than you.

SAMUEL

(*offended*) I'm splitting a gut. Has it started raining again?

MARTHA

No.

SAMUEL

What about your hair?

DANNY

Did you go for a swim in the river? With the volunteers? (*MARTHA smiles.*) I envy you. Today, that's all people could talk about … I would've liked to join them but my duty was here.

MARTHA

They're still there, if you want—

SAMUEL

Don't corrupt him.

DANNY

"If Danny joined the others his age, he'd become careless and ill-bred, living for nothing but night-long orgies, drunk on illicit elixirs with powerful erectile effects. He would entwine his body with the others', lending his tongue to other tongues, an affront to his juvenile splendours."

SAMUEL

Where do you get ideas like that?

DANNY

That's your piece about me.

MARTHA
    He's adorable.

SAMUEL
    Do you realize he's reconstructed fourteen texts?

MARTHA
    Fourteen!

SAMUEL
    At this rate, a year from now—

DANNY
    Every one I transcribe lightens the load on my
    memory.

SAMUEL
    Fourteen texts reborn!

MARTHA
    A miracle!

SAMUEL
    I feel like celebrating.

MARTHA
    Two miracles? How do you do it, Danny?

DANNY
    It must be because of my wings.

SAMUEL
    I feel like dancing.

MARTHA
    Are you serious?

SAMUEL
    Show me some dance steps, Martha.

MARTHA
    Which ones?

SAMUEL

I don't care.

MARTHA

I'm not sure…

SAMUEL

Steps so I can dance like Monica Bacio.

MARTHA

Your collar's all twisted again.

SAMUEL

Stop fussing. Show me a dance and sing.

DANNY

All we have to do is write: "Mr. Samuel Dances and Sings" and everything is possible.

SAMUEL

Go ahead. Write: "Samuel is dancing. Samuel is singing."

DANNY

(*closing his eyes*) "Samuel is having fun!" That's my title. "His stiff legs and his awkward arms start moving, and caught up in a devilish frenzy—"

SAMUEL

(*dancing any old way*) "—the old gentleman started writhing around—"

MARTHA

"—a terrible sight to behold!" How do you expect me to show you if you don't stay still?

SAMUEL

Go ahead! Show me.

MARTHA

Stand with your feet parallel. Cross your right foot in front of the left and say "one."

SAMUEL

One.

MARTHA

Again. Now, step back with the left foot and say "two."

SAMUEL

I step back with the left foot and I say two.

MARTHA

Good. Now, one and two.

SAMUEL

One and two.

MARTHA

Then you step to the side, spin around and you say "three." Repeat that three times.

SAMUEL

One, two and three. Sing.

MARTHA

(*singing in Italian and dancing with* SAM)
"Veglia su di noi / la luna cupa"
(*The moon watches over us*)
"Come sui piccoli / vcglia la lupa"
(*Like mother wolf over her cubs will fuss*)
"Veglia su di noi / la luna quatta"
(*The moon watches over us*)
"Come il manicomio / veglia sulla matta"
(*Like guardian angel over incubus*)
"La luna cupa / La luna quatta" (*repeat … *)

DANNY

(*his eyes closed*) "Danny is flying! Flying!" I have to close my eyes to see myself fly. But when I open them, I'm still pinned to the ground. Words can create all sorts of images, but you have to close your eyes to see them. Why can't we see them with our eyes open? Why are we never what we write? Why can't we become metaphors? Why can't we be allegories or figures of speech? Why does it make me so sad? I wish I could enter my writing. Then I could fly and rise above everything, just to understand life and see it in a single image. When I'm too close, I find life too complicated. If we could become what we write, it would be extraordinary. We have to try to become what we write, Mr. Samuel.

SAMUEL

We'll work on that, Danny, but right now it's getting late.

DANNY

Some day I'm going to write: "I am flying" and I will fly.

SAMUEL

You're right. We have to enter our writing.

DANNY

(*tenderly, touching his cheek*) I'll stay here. You can take tomorrow morning off if you want.

SAMUEL

Why?

DANNY

To recover from too much dancing, maybe?

SAMUEL

I don't need to recover.

DANNY

You can take the whole day off if you want.

SAMUEL

(*sarcastically*) The week, the month, the year, if you want??

DANNY

I don't need your help to put everything back in order.

SAMUEL

What do you mean?

DANNY

You make too many mistakes … even on your own texts. There were two important omissions in your restoration of "The First Day of School."

SAMUEL

Impossible.

DANNY

You omitted: "Fearful, the children silently waited to be assigned their new teacher … " and "Once the teacher's name had been pronounced, a rush of relief or anxiety, depending upon his reputation."

SAMUEL

I'll just add that.

DANNY

I'll do it tomorrow.

SAMUEL

It's my text!

DANNY

I'd write it differently: "The children, imprisoned in time, chained to the shackles of learning, sat mute and obedient, waiting to be assigned a new tyrant."

SAMUEL

That's not what I wrote.

DANNY

That's what I'd write in your place.

SAMUEL

(*to MARTHA*) You hear that! He's correcting me!

DANNY

Your sentences are too tame.

SAMUEL

How dare you lecture me?

DANNY

Those are your own teachings. I just want to apply them.

SAMUEL

Are you serious?

DANNY

There are also serious problems with your filing system.

SAMUEL

I let the devil enter our circle.

DANNY

It's not right for Anita Plourde to be so far from Charles Lapointe.

SAMUEL

They weren't close.

DANNY

They had a bastard child together.

MARTHA

(*surprised*) Who did?

DANNY

One day, under the East Bridge, I heard them talking. And then there's Jean-Marc Johnson who should be next to Louis-Paul Picard.

SAMUEL

They couldn't stand each other. Everybody knows that.

DANNY

Except when they were alone in the woods together.

MARTHA

Are there lots of errors like that?

DANNY

A few, yes.

SAMUEL

(*furious*) Tell us! Tell us the errors, Mr. Know-it-all!

DANNY

Your voice is resuming its usual habits.

SAMUEL

Finish what you started to say.

DANNY

(*to SAMUEL*) I think you're in the wrong place in the filing system.

SAMUEL

Me, in the wrong place? EXPLAIN!

DANNY

You'll kick me out.

SAMUEL

Kick you out? Who's kicking whom out??!

MARTHA

Explain, Danny.

DANNY

I don't understand what you're doing next to your wife in the files. (*Beat.*)

SAMUEL

She was my wife!

DANNY

I don't think she wanted to be next to you.

SAMUEL

How dare you say that to me?

DANNY

(*handing him a text, which he recites by heart*) "'A Woman Sacrificed.' This will be my last text. Tomorrow, I'm going to die. Memories have finally devoured my bones. I don't want to write in the past tense anymore, or talk about myself in the third person. I don't want to get stuck in 'the old days!' Samuel, you cheated on me with nostalgia. A greedy mistress, nostalgia robbed me of everything. Tomorrow, I'm going to risk your violence and write to our children who left to live far from us too long ago."

SAMUEL

(*violent*) You can go join the others your age now. You can tell them you found "the flaw." Isn't that why you're here? Go ahead! Go tell them I was a bad husband, a bad father … Is that the kind of writing you're interested in? Is that what you want to write about? Other people's mistakes? (*Beat.*) I thought you were talented. I'd forgotten that talent is the mother of laziness and the sister of arrogance. (*Beat.*) "To enter our writing!" A person has to write something worthwhile before he can give lessons to others. I would've helped you restructure your piece. I would've suggested some cuts. You would've objected. A real battle. We would've had a real battle. But no, you turn your nose up at everything and you criticize, you criticize and make comments. (*Beat.*) Human beings can't fly and will never fly. Human beings are pinned to the ground. They hurt those closest to them and they cloud their memories. Period! I should've known better. I should've known better. (*Silence.*)

MARTHA

Let me fix your collar.

SAMUEL

(*shoving MARTHA away violently*) This is no time for that!

MARTHA

You hurt me, Sam. You hurt me.

DANNY

If we could become what we write, you could bring your wife back to life and you could console her. I have tears for words. Tears. (*DANNY exits.*)

MARTHA

You hurt me.

SAMUEL

What are you waiting for? Why don't you go join Claire now?

MARTHA

My wrist is broken.

SAMUEL

Young people are traitors.

MARTHA

You broke my wrist.

He exits.

MARTHA

(*resigned to staying with* SAMUEL) "Martha had carefully packed Claire's belongings in a box. One by one, the heaviest things at the bottom, the most delicate on top. Just as she was about to pack the imaginary love notes, the ones never written, the ones that should leave no trace, she stopped. 'My dearest, my sweetest, my darling ... ' She imagined herself caressing the paper as she had so often caressed her friend's cheek. She pressed all the unwritten words, the imaginary letters, to her heart, and, resigned to seal their fate, she closed the box." My title: "The Parting of Two Friends."

Scene 13

CLAIRE

(*her hair wet*) If I bury her cat, somebody will find him. With everyone digging up everything, searching for lost objects, somebody's sure to find him. If I throw him in the river, he'll wash ashore somewhere. If I burn him, the smoke will alert everyone. I have to make him vanish. It's the only solution. If I could rewrite my life, I'd skin him, meticulously. I'd give a real tug when I got to the part around his head. Then I'd pluck out his fur and scatter it to the four winds. I'd be surprised to discover that a little animal like him has pink, tender flesh that melts in the mouth. "*God provides food, the devil seasons it.*" *The Parish Newsletter.* If I could rewrite my life, I'd eat Martha's cat and I'd become a figure of speech.

Scene 14

In the cemetery, at night. WILLIAM *joins* SAM.

WILLIAM

"The river flowed in the background at the cemetery, just below the village. Clad in dark, the flock of crows in mourning followed the coffin."

SAMUEL

"Everyone was thinking of the day when they would have to become, for one or the other, corpse or gravedigger ... "

SAMUEL AND WILLIAM

" ... for one or the other."

WILLIAM

Martha wrote that one.

SAMUEL

I just broke her wrist.

WILLIAM

I know.

SAMUEL

I kicked Danny out of the writing room.

WILLIAM

I know that, too.

SAMUEL

And you want to kick me out of the ruins of my house.

WILLIAM

You shouldn't look at it that way.

SAMUEL

If you've come to make me sign your damn papers, you can go back where you came from.

WILLIAM

    I needed a breath of fresh air.

SAMUEL

    In the cemetery?

WILLIAM

    There's air here, too, isn't there?

SAMUEL

    The papers for the house are sticking out of your pocket, you're not a very good liar.

WILLIAM

    And what did you come here for?

SAMUEL

    I came to talk to my wife.

WILLIAM

    Where is your wife?

SAMUEL

    Somewhere at the bottom of the river. The flood even swept away the graves.

WILLIAM

    I'm sorry.

SAMUEL

    I miss her.

WILLIAM

    If Dorothy ever left me, it would kill me.

SAMUEL

    (*ironically*) You know how to console a man. Aren't you going to say hello to our old mayor? He's over there, at the foot of that tree.

WILLIAM

    (*nodding a greeting*) Mr. Mayor.

SAMUEL

With both wives at his side. His first wife is worse off than the other.

WILLIAM

She wasn't in such great shape when she was alive. "As soon as the mourning period for his first wife ended, the mayor announced his wedding … "

SAMUEL

"And made his fiancée big with child, before he led her down the aisle."

WILLIAM

The more I look at the mayor, the more I think we should be cremated. They've got some good package deals, you know. They take care of everything. Everything from announcing the news to the family to the buffet after the funeral. Or you can order à la carte.

SAMUEL

If you don't choose "announcing the news to the family," the buffet must be a lot cheaper.

WILLIAM

What do you mean?

SAMUEL

If you don't announce the death, no one will come.

> *WILLIAM laughs.*

SAMUEL

Finally somebody laughs.

WILLIAM

Come with us. We'll learn some new sports.

SAMUEL

Don't you think it's a bit late for pole vaulting?

WILLIAM

There'll be cultural activities.

SAMUEL

In nature, when animals grow old, they become
more and more discreet. They don't drive around
in a yellow school bus singing Monica Bacio songs
at the top of their lungs.

WILLIAM

Travel.

SAMUEL

Pushing our walkers up church steps.

WILLIAM

You could do volunteer work.

SAMUEL

We'll be so busy with all our activities, we won't see
death come sneaking up on us. And in the middle
of a dance, snap!, she will have offered us her arm.
(*WILLIAM goes to sit down.*) Don't sit down there!

WILLIAM

Why not?

SAMUEL

Because that's my place.

WILLIAM

How can you be in two places at once?

SAMUEL

I paid for that spot ages ago. The stone has
disappeared, but that's my plot. The only thing
missing was the date.

WILLIAM

You might want to die here lost in your memories,
but I still have a wife to take care of. Sign the

papers for me. You can do what you want with your share of the money, but you can't decide for us. I don't believe we came into this world to make other people sweat it out!

SAMUEL

What are we here for, William?

WILLIAM

I don't know. But you could make the search for the answer more pleasant.

DANNY

(*as he enters, glowing, almost nude*) I made love, Mr. Samuel. I made love, Mr. William. I finally made love. My title: "Danny-the-lonely-child Finally Made Love." "The master's anger made me sad. She was standing off from the others, wearing, as her only jewel, a smile. The moon made her skin look even whiter. She said: Come here, let me console you. I got undressed and joined her in the water. I was cold to the tip of my wings. I told her how I'd eaten all the hosts. She said: I don't go to church. I told her: You're pretty, anyway. Our shoulders brushed against each other. She asked me to say something gentle to her. I whispered:
A woman lay on a veranda taking a rest
Dozing, one shoulder bared
The breeze, like a lover, revealed her breast.
What's your name? Raven, I said. Noah's raven, the one who flew away and never found land. I am Dove, the dove who brought back the olive branch. Gabriel, who appeared to the Virgin. Icarus, from the sun. Phoenix, risen from the ashes. Mercury, bearer of glad tidings. No. I'm more than all that. I am Danny. Danny, from the

writing room. Some day, I'll be the guardian. And our shoulders, again … Can I caress your stomach? Please say yes. Are you afraid of me? My parents say I'm handsome. Easy for them to say. Their skin looks like ripples in the sand. 'Ripples in the sand,' that's a metaphor. Do you think I'm handsome? Do you want to touch me first? Feel my stomach, like a valley ploughed in spring. My neck, as solid as a tree trunk. My arms as hard as rock. Those are all metaphors. Do you want to touch me where all obsessions lie? Yes, touch. Touch, touch, touch … It feels good. Why did you touch me? To forget someone else? Why did it feel good? Why do I want you to do it again? I'll never touch anyone else. I'll never forget you. Can I touch you where all words are born? Today, Danny entered the writing room and he made love."

WILLIAM

Big day!

SAMUEL

You'll have to rework all that for me. It lacks mystery.

DANNY

I know. There are too many "I's" and "she said's." I'd be glad to rework all that with her.

SAMUEL

(*to WILLIAM*) What do we do, once we've written our love, once we've written our children, once we've written our dreams and our disappointments? Do we spend the rest of our days re-reading our lives? Or do we rewrite it all, to nurture our illusions? What do we do?

WILLIAM

(*reciting*) "In conclusion, when setting his traps, a trapper should never forget that animals have an advantage over us: their sense of smell. The small-game hunter should avoid artificial scents. Avoid all soaps, perfumes and most of all, the smell of gas."

SAMUEL

Give me the papers so I can sign them. (*SAM signs the papers.*)

WILLIAM

Today I spoke to an old man on my cell phone. He told me: "Don't try to hold onto anything, let go, that's all." We'll come say goodbye tomorrow morning. (*WILLIAM exits.*)

SAMUEL

(*to DANNY*) I need your help.

DANNY

Here I am.

SAMUEL

It's time for me to enter my writing.

DANNY

We need a title.

SAMUEL

Helen. My wife's name was Helen.

DANNY

My title: "Helen and Sam." And it will be a reunion.

SAMUEL

Go on, I'm not afraid.

SAMUEL gets undressed slowly, while DANNY
improvises, his eyes closed. SAMUEL disappears into
the water in the course of DANNY's story.

DANNY

"I followed old Samuel from above. The moonlight
glowed on his white body. He walked along the
river. 'Where are you? Where are you? Let your
tears guide my steps.' And deep sobs could be
heard from the waterfall upstream. He followed
the sound of his siren's tears. When he reached
the rapids, he walked into the river slowly. And
under the water, he found the grave of his
beloved. Her black dress for eternity swirled in the
currents of the stream. Her arms reached out to
him. Her hair swayed like a field of golden wheat
in the wind. She was as lovely as their first spring.
Her sad eyes were smiling. She gestured for him to
come closer. They didn't speak, as the depths
watched over them. First, he kissed her wrist and
the bandage wrapped so tight for so long fell off,
swirling until it disappeared in the waves. Then,
with Herculean strength, commanding his fragile
bones and frail muscles, he tore his wife from the
mud. It was as if he uprooted her. And as he
walked out of the water, he let out a great cry. He
woke the thrushes and the robins, the titmice and
the finches, and all the birds joined me in flight.
He carried his wife for miles, circling all the
boulders, striding over the chasms. He entered the
village triumphant, like a man defying destiny. In
his wake, the church rose up again, the bridges
returned to their pillars, the river retreated to its
bed. The curtains always drawn to harbour gossip
opened in compassion. All the elderly watched this

giant who, after years in mourning, was finally bringing his wife home. And they were young again. Their ripples of sand were erased and the laughter of children filled the air. The manuscripts washed out to sea were now read, celebrated and sung by all humanity. And, when he reached the threshold of his house, the old man's knees buckled. He fell. His heart, bursting to excess, ached. His wife leaned over him. 'Tell me what's wrong?' and the old man replied: 'I want to know who will take care of the writing room.' That's when he raised his hand to the sky. I thought he was calling me. I didn't know whether I should fetch a pen or a host. And then, his heart, a second time. Indomitable, the flow of blood broke all the dams. Uncontrollable, another flood wreaked havoc in his chest and the crimson wave swept his life away." (*Beat.*) I'll sit down here and be Mrs. Claire: "The cat's got your tongue … At night, all cats are grey … when the cat's away, the mouse will play … Like a cat on a hot tin roof … To play cat and mouse … " After trying all the figures of speech, Claire finally told Martha outright: "I want to live with you and your cat is dead. Do you want me to say it in a different order: Your cat is dead and I want to live with you." "Sam is dead and I can live with you. I can live with you and Sam is dead." That's Mrs. Martha: "Metaphors are figures of speech that mask lies. We say *Golden Age* for old age. We say *The Journey's End* for death. *Wisdom* for disillusionment. *The Twilight Years* for the loss of hope. *The Gateway to Paradise* for an asylum." And Mrs. Dorothy: "A dress for eternity. It will be white and lowcut. It will be daring, transparent and gay. I want my white hair." And I'll be Mr. William: "Our immortality is our children ... and our children's children ... and our children's children's children ... That is the true rewrite ... Tomorrow, when my grandchildren put their arms around my neck, I'll be immortal." And I will be Danny-the-lonely-child, and I'll take my turn as guardian of the writing room.

The End

AGMV Marquis

MEMBER OF SCABRINI MEDIA

Quebec, Canada
2004